STIR UP THE GIFTS

Empowering Believers for Victorious Living & Ministry Tasks

WORKBOOK & STUDY GUIDE

The Gift of God is as Precious as a Jewel ... Proverbs 17:8

George O. McCalep, Jr., PhD.

TABLE OF CONTENTS

ABOUT THE STIR UP THE GIFTS WORKBOOK/STUDY GUIDE

The Stir Up The Gifts Workbook/Study Guide was designed to be used as a part of the Stir Up The Gifts textbook curriculum. If you are not taking a Stir Up The Gifts course you may still find the workbook to be effective for individual usage along with the Stir Up The Gifts textbook.

INTRODUCTION

STIR UP
THE GIFTS

In What Ways Could We Be Ignorant Regarding Spiritual Gifts?

Not knowing that
Spiritual Gifts exist

Unaware of the
Spiritual Gifts we possess

Not Knowing Where
to use Spiritual Gifts

*Thinking Spiritual Gifts
are something they are not

*see activity on page 6 regarding Spiritual Gift Confusion

SPIRITUAL GIFTS DEFINED

Directions:
Turn your Bible to the Scripture References below to define Spiritual Gifts *(The Living Bible preferred)*. Use the space provided below to write your definition.

SPIRITUAL GIFTS ARE: supernatural

I Cor. 12:4 –   distributed by The

I Cor. 12:11 –   to every

I Peter 4:10 –   according to God's grace

                                                    and design for the

I Cor. 12:7 –   of the body of Christ.

I Corin. 12

See the bottom of page 7 for answer to Spiritual Gifts definition.

Triune Being

	Spiritual Gifts	Holy Spirit
v. 5	Ministries	Jesus Christ
v. 6	Personalities	God the Father

SPIRITUAL GIFT CONFUSION

Directions:
1.) Choose one of the definitions from page 6 or 7 of your textbook.
2.) Read and discuss your chosen definition with your group.
3.) Next, select the group activity below that matches the definition your group chose earlier.

GROUP I – FRUIT OF THE SPIRIT

1.) Based upon what you have read on page 6 of your textbook regarding the Fruit of the Spirit, give an overall definition of its meaning.

_____

_____

2.) What is the difference in the Fruit of the Spirit and Spiritual Gifts?

_____

GROUP II – SPIRITUAL ADMONISHMENT

1.) Based upon what you have read on page 7 of your textbook regarding Spiritual Admonishment, give an overall definition of it's meaning.

_____

_____

2.) What is the difference in Spiritual Admonishment and Spiritual Gifts?

_____

GROUP III – MEMBERS OF THE CLERGY

1.) Based upon what you have read on page 7 of your textbook regarding members of the clergy, give an overall definition of its meaning.

_____

_____

2.) What is the difference in members of the clergy and Spiritual Gifts?

_____

GROUP IV– NATURAL ABILITIES

1.) Based upon what you have read on page 6 regarding Natural Abilities, give an overall definition of its meaning.

_____

2.) What is the difference in natural abilities and Spiritual Gifts?

Natural abilities (talents) glorify self.
Spiritual gifts glorify God.
Using your talents to drain you.
" " spir. gifts " energize you.

THREE WAYS IN WHICH TO TEST THE AUTHENTICITY OF SPIRITUAL GIFTS
(Is this really a Spiritual Gift?)

Directions:

1.)   Choose one of the test definitions on page 8 of your textbook regarding how to test Spiritual Gifts and discuss it with your group.

2.)   Next, select the scenario below that matches the test definition your group chose earlier and try to determine if the test definition proves the person's Gift in the scenario to be a Spiritual Gift or not.

GROUP I – TEST OF DOCTRINE

Mr. Jones is a very inspiring public school 12th grade teacher who has been recognized throughout the community for uplifting the youth and motivating them to succeed. Mr. Jones, after hearing about prestigious Greenforest Church, recently joined there and has already been asked by several people to join in teaching youth Sunday School, so he does.

One day as the pastor and some of the visitors are passing by Mr. Jones' class, they overhear him discussing the trinity. He very boldly encourages the students that as long as they believe in a higher power other than themselves then the rest of their belief is covered by just simply believing that there is a God, whether He has revealed Himself as one, two, or three persons.

GROUP II – THE TEST OF KNOWLEDGE, LOVE & ORDER

One Sunday as the pastor was preaching, Sis. Jenkins, caught up in the spirit, jumped up, laid hands on the person sitting next to her and began to speak in an unknown tongue. This went on for two minutes and when she was done laying hands on the person, she sat back down and praised the Lord out loudly, for two more minutes. By the time her praise was over, so was the pastor's sermon. *She might have the gift, but she used it out of order.*

GROUP III – THE FRUIT TEST

Bro. Jerry is a very energetic leader of the youth ministry at his church. He constantly stresses God's design for sex within the context of a marriage to his youth. Bro. Jerry, however, **lives with** the mother of his children. *The gift is there. The ministry should be rejected.*

ANSWER: The Spiritual Gifts Definition from page 5 Should Read as Follows:

Spiritual Gifts are **special abilities** (1 Cor. 12:4) distributed by **THE HOLY SPIRIT** (1 Cor. 12:11) to **every believer** according to God's grace and design (1 Peter 4:10) for the **common good** (1 Cor. 12: 7) of the body of Christ.

CHAPTER 1

Stir Up The Gift of God (LOVE)

It's All About Love

The love of God is the source of the Gifts and the love of God will be what remains when Spiritual Gifts have vanished.

"No Love" equals "no motivation." And "no motivation" results in "no service."

God says stir up the Gift (singular), yet there are many Gifts. Just as He speaks of the fruit (singular) of The Spirit, yet there are many fruits. Why? Because love is both the Gift and the fruit from which all Gifts and fruits spring forth.

WHAT IS LOVE?

Directions:
Look up scripture references to see what The Bible has to say about love.

_____

I Corinthians 13:4-7

_____

I Peter 4:8

_____

I John 4:18

_____

I John 4:8

_____

John 15:13

_____

Galatians 5:22

WHEN/WHO/HOW TO LOVE

Directions:
Choose one of the group activities below using the scripture references assigned to each to answer the questions assigned to each group's activity.

GROUP I – WHEN SHOULD YOU LOVE?
(Ephesians 4:31-32)

1..) _____

2.) _____

3.) _____

4.) _____

5.) _____

6.) _____

7.) _____

GROUP II – WHO SHOULD YOU LOVE?

1..) _____
(John 17:6)

2.) _____
(Ephesians 6:18)

3.) _____
(Mark 12:31 & Matthew 19:19)

4.) _____
(Galatians 2:10, Acts 6:1-3, Hosea 1:2)

5.) _____
(Romans 12:20 & Matthew 5:44)

GROUP III – HOW TO LOVE?

1..) _____
(Galatians 5:6 & Matthew 9:21-22)

2.) _____
(Matthew 25:1-4)

3.) _____
(1 John 4:18)

4.) _____
(Isaiah 53:7 & Proverbs 17:28)

STUDY QUESTIONS – CHAPTER I

1.)   What is the greatest Gift of all Gifts? This one sparks all the other Gifts?

_____

2.)   What is the main point of I Corinthians 13 (the love chapter)?

_____

_____

3.)   List the seven things that love will do.

  1.) _____   2.) _____   3.) _____
  4.) _____   5.) _____   6.) _____
  7.) _____   8.) _____

4.)   List the 8 things that love will not do.

  1.) _____   2.) _____   3.) _____
  4.) _____   5.) _____   6.) _____
  7.) _____   8.) _____

5.)   Complete the following scriptural truth sentences.

  Faith works by _____.

  God is _____.

  Love _____ a multitude of _____.

  It has not yet been revealed _____.

  We must therefore diligently follow _____.

  Love is both the _____ and the _____ from which all others spring forth.

  Bondage is a product of _____.

  Freedom is a child of _____.

6.)   Love is both a _____ and a _____.

7.)   What will happen if you stir up the Gift of love?

8.)   What will happen if you fail to stir up the Gift of love?

9.)   What does Mother Teresa call "love in action?"

10.) What is the purpose of Spiritual Gifts?

Answers on page 64

CHAPTER 2

Overcoming Intimidation & The Spirit of Fear

9 PRINCIPLES TO OVERCOMING THE SPIRIT OF INTIMIDATION & FEAR

Use the key code below to find the 9 principles to overcoming the spirit of intimidation and fear.

A	B	C	D	E	F	G	H	I	J	K	L	M
07	01	24	05	26	13	22	19	17	20	16	08	23

N	O	P	Q	R	S	T	U	V	W	X	Y	Z
10	21	03	18	04	12	15	25	11	09	14	06	02

___ ___ ___ ___ ___ ___ ___ ___ ___   ___ ___ ___   ___ ___ ___ ___ ___
04 26 24 21 22 10 17 02 26   15 19 26   26 10 26 23 06

___ ___ ___ ___ ___ ___ ___   ___ ___ ___ ___ ___ ___ ___   ___ ___ ___ ___ ___
07 01 07 10 05 21 10   24 21 23 13 21 04 15   02 21 10 26 12

___ ___ ___ ___   ___ ___ ___   ___ ___ ___ ___ ___ ___ ___ ___ ___ ___   ___ ___ ___   ___ ___ ___ ___ ___   ___ ___
16 10 21 09   07 10 05   26 14 03 26 04 17 26 10 24 26   15 19 26   03 21 09 26 04   21 13

___ ___ ___ ___ ___ ___
03 04 07 17 12 26

___ ___ ___ ___ ___ ___   ___ ___ ___   ___ ___ ___ ___ ___   ___ ___ ___   ___ ___ ___ ___   ___ ___ ___
12 15 07 04 11 26   15 19 26   13 08 26 12 19   07 10 05   13 26 26 05   15 19 26

___ ___ ___ ___ ___ ___
12 03 17 04 17 15

___ ___ ___ ___   ___ ___ ___ ___   ___ ___ ___ ___   ___ ___ ___ ___ ___ ___ ___
12 15 07 06   07 09 07 06   13 04 21 23   07 11 26 04 07 22 26

___ ___ ___ ___   ___ ___ ___ ___ ___   ___ ___ ___   ___ ___ ___ ___ ___   ___ ___ ___ ___
08 17 11 26   07 01 21 11 26   15 19 26   12 10 07 16 26   08 17 10 26

___ ___ ___ ___   ___ ___ ___ ___   ___ ___ ___ ___   ___ ___ ___ ___ ___ ___ ___ ___ ___
12 15 07 06   07 09 07 06   13 04 21 23   19 21 08 08 06 09 21 21 05

___ ___ ___ ___ ___ ___ ___ ___ ___ ___ ___ ___
24 19 04 17 12 15 17 07 10 17 15 06

___ ___ ___ ___ ___ ___ ___   ___   ___ ___ ___ ___ ___ ___   ___ ___ ___ ___ ___ ___ ___ ___ ___ ___
05 26 11 26 08 21 03   07   03 21 03 26 06 26   23 26 10 15 07 08 17 15 06

OVERCOMING EVIL WITH GOOD

Directions:
Use the scripture references below and discuss with your group how each scripture reference promotes overcoming evil with good.

GROUP I – ROMANS 12:19

_____

_____

Romans 12:19 Dearly beloved, avenge not yourselves, but rather give place unto wrath: for it is written, Vengeance is mine; I will repay, saith the Lord.

GROUP II – ROMANS 12:21

_____

_____

Romans 12:21 Be not overcome of evil, but overcome evil with good.

GROUP III – HEBREWS 12:3-4

_____

_____

Hebrews 12:3-4 If you want to keep from becoming faint-hearted and weary, think about his patience as sinful men did such terrible things to him. After all, you have never yet struggled against sin and temptation until you sweat great drops of blood.

WHO/WHAT DO YOU FEAR?

Directions:

Complete the Self Discovery Exercise below. The purpose of this activity is to recognize those things you fear or are intimidated by, particularly those things that hinder you from using your Spiritual Gift(s).

Past	Present	Future

STUDY QUESTIONS – CHAPTER 2

1.) Intimidation is the servant of the _____.

2.) Perfect _____ casts out fear.

3.) Since intimidation is caused by fear, how can intimidation be overcome?

_____

_____

4.) Where does the spirit of fear come from? _____.

5.) What can we accomplish with the weapon of praise? _____.

6.) Identify three areas where you rest in your own comfort zone rather than breaking free to do God's will.

_____   _____   _____

7.) What happens when you move away from loving God first in your life?

_____

8.) What does the author mean when he says "starve the flesh and feed the spirit"?

_____

_____

9.) What does the snake line mean as it relates to character?

_____

_____

10.) What does the author mean by Hollywood Christianity?

_____

11.) What does the author mean by a Popeye Mentality?

_____

12.) According to Paul, what was Timothy's problem?

_____

Answers on page 64

CHAPTER 3

Reviving Spiritual Gifts

PRINCIPLE POINTS REGARDING THE REVIVAL OF SPIRITUAL GIFTS

EZEKIEL 37: 1-14

The analogy of the dry bones lying lifeless and dormant until The Spirit of God revives them.

~ ~ ~

UNUSED SPIRITUAL GIFTS

An important prerequisite to reviving Spiritual Gifts is acknowledging that you actually have not been using them and therefore, they must be lying dormant. Since all saints have been given at least one Gift, chances are, if you don't know what it is, it is unused.

~ ~ ~

THE NEED IS URGENT

Spiritual Gifts in the Church today are not being used to their full potential. Imagine what would happen if every believer's Gifts were revived and put into active service in the Church today.

~ ~ ~

THE HOLY SPIRIT'S WORK IN REVIVAL

The Holy Spirit can revive the Gifts if we allow Him in. We must learn to work with Him as he breathes the breath of life back into the Gifts. He has deposited the Gifts in the Church to further God's cause here on earth.

~ ~ ~

STIR UP YOUR OWN GIFTS

God will not stir up the Gifts if you don't want Him to. You have to take the first step. Call on The Lord and The Holy Spirit to help you. But you must start stirring the smoldering ashes yourself. Add some more kindling and stir it up.

WRITE THE VISION

Directions:

Based upon Dr. McCalep's "vision for Spiritual Gifts" from pages 51-52 of your textbook, use the format below and write the vision you have for your Spiritual Gift(s).

I have a dream that one day my Spiritual Gift(s) of _____
_____ will be stirred up and revived for the task of ministry. I know that we are not all called to preach or pastor, but we are all called to minister and we have all been Gifted for the task of ministry.

I have a dream that I will become more than a conqueror when it comes to using my Gift(s). I have a dream that _____
_____
_____
will happen because of the discovery of my Spiritual Gift(s).

I have a dream that my Spiritual Gift(s) of _____,
given by God, will rise up from the pews and seek to find gainful employment.

I have a dream that my Spiritual Gift(s) of _____
will be used always in God's love.

I have a dream that if I use my Spiritual Gift(s) of _____
that God will allow my Gift(s) to grow in the task of ministry by:
_____
_____

I have a dream that I will no longer neglect my Spiritual Gift(s) but will stir up, employ, and empower my Spiritual Gift(s) to the furtherance and glory of God's kingdom.

Yes I, _____ have a dream!
            (NAME)

STUDY QUESTIONS – CHAPTER 3

1.)　What happens to Spiritual Gifts unused?

　　　_____

2.)　What is the purpose of revival in the church?

　　　_____

3.)　We need a fresh filling of _____ to revive our Gifts.

4.)　How does the Ezekiel 37 illustration relate to Spiritual Gifts?

　　　_____

　　　_____

5.)　Everyone in the Body of Christ has at least _____ Spiritual Gift.

6.)　Who is the power behind all Spiritual Gifts? _____.

Answers on page 65

CHAPTER 4

Being Good Stewards of Spiritual Gifts

THE HEART OF A GOOD STEWARD

There are 7 words hidden in this puzzle that defines the heart of a good steward. See if you can find them.

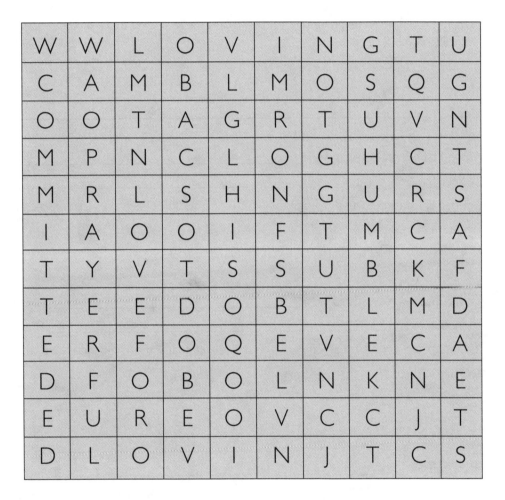

W	W	L	O	V	I	N	G	T	U
C	A	M	B	L	M	O	S	Q	G
O	O	T	A	G	R	T	U	V	N
M	P	N	C	L	O	G	H	C	T
M	R	L	S	H	N	G	U	R	S
I	A	O	O	I	F	T	M	C	A
T	Y	V	T	S	S	U	B	K	F
T	E	E	D	O	B	T	L	M	D
E	R	F	O	Q	E	V	E	C	A
D	F	O	B	O	L	N	K	N	E
E	U	R	E	O	V	C	C	J	T
D	L	O	V	I	N	J	T	C	S

Words can be found at the bottom of page 25 but first try to find them on your own.

RECONCILIATION OUTLINE

Directions:

Use the outline below to identify relationships you need to reconcile, as described on page 57 of your textbook, that are hindering you from being a good steward of your Spiritual Gift(s).

~ ~ ~

Therefore if thou bring thy Gift to the altar, and there rememberest that thy brother has ought against thee; leave there thy Gift before the altar, and go thy way; first be reconciled to thy brother, and then come and offer thy Gift - Matt. 5:24.

~ ~ ~

I acknowledge that my relationship with _____ is in need of reconciliation due to _____. I also know that If I desire to use my Spiritual Gift(s) to its full effect that I must reconcile this relationship immediately.

I acknowledge that my relationship with _____ is in need of reconciliation due to _____. I also know that If I desire to use my Spiritual Gift(s) to its full effect that I must reconcile this relationship immediately.

I acknowledge that my relationship with _____ is in need of reconciliation due to _____. I also know that If I desire to use my Spiritual Gift(s) to its full effect that I must reconcile this relationship immediately.

AVAILABILITY OUTLINE

Directions:

Make a list of those things that keep you from being available in using your Spiritual Gift(s), as described on page 58 of your textbook.

1.) _____

2.) _____

3.) _____

4.) _____

5.) _____

6.) _____

7.) _____

Words to puzzle on page 23
The Heart of a Good Steward is: Committed, Consistent, Humble, Loving, Prayerful, Steadfast, & Watchful

STUDY QUESTIONS – CHAPTER 4

1.)   What is a steward? _____

2.)   What does it mean to be a good steward? _____

3.)   Give a summary sentence for each of the following characteristics of a good steward:

Acknowledgement – _____

Reconciliation – _____

Availability – _____

Motivation – _____

Spiritual Maturity – _____

Sacrifice – _____

Accountability – _____

Faithfulness – _____

4.)   What does Jesus say about faithfulness and neglect of the Gifts?

_____

_____

5.)   Describe the significance of service as it relates to Spiritual Gifts.

_____

Answers on page 65

CHAPTER 5

Discovering Your Spiritual Gift(s) & Ministry Profile

YOUR MINISTRY PROFILE

- ## **S**piritual Gifts
  What am I Gifted to do?

- ## **H**eart
  What do I love to do? (Passion)

- ## **A**bilities
  What do I do well now?

- ## **P**ersonality temperment
  Why do I act the way I do?

- ## **E**xperience
  Why do I perceive as I do?

SPIRITUAL GIFTS OF THE NEW TESTAMENT

Directions:

See how well you know the Spiritual Gifts of the New Testament by matching the Gifts in Column A to the descriptions in Column B. Use the blanks provided to write your answers.

Column A

1.) _____ Administration

2.) _____ Prophecy

3.) _____ Wisdom

4.) _____ Creative Communication

5.) _____ Tongues

6.) _____ Knowledge

7.) _____ Miracles

8.) _____ Faith

9.) _____ Shepherding

10.) _____ Healings

11.) _____ Teaching

Column B

A. To know. The divine enablement to bring truth to the body of Christ through biblical insight.

B. To speak God's truth. The divine enablement to warn of God's immediate or future judgment.

C. To trust. The divine enablement to stand on God's promises with confidence.

D. To organize. The divine enablement to create order out of organizational chaos.

E. To instruct. The divine enablement to communicate biblical truth that inspires greater obedience to God's word.

F. To apply God's word. The divine enablement to provide given solutions in the midst of conflict.

G. Unknown language. The divine enablement to speak, worship, or pray in an unknown language.

H. To do powerful deeds. The divine enablement to perform the supernatural.

I. To nurture a flock. The divine enablement to care for and provide guidance to the Body of Christ.

J. To restore. The divine enablement to restore to wholeness.

K. To communicate artistically. The

SPIRITUAL GIFTS OF THE NEW TESTAMENT (CONT'D)

Column A

12.) _____ Hospitality

13.) _____ Intercessory
              Prayer

14.) _____ Interpretation
              of Tongues

15.) _____ Giving

16.) _____ Leadership

17.) _____ Mercy

18.) _____ Helps

19.) _____ Craftsmanship

20.) _____ Exhortation

21.) _____ Evangelism

22.) _____ Discernment

23.) _____ Apostleship

Column B

L.   To be sent. The divine enablement to establish new churches or ministries.

M.   To design. The divine enablement to create or construct items to be used for ministry.

N.   To make distinction. The divine enablement to identify deceptions and distinguish truth.

O.   To plead. The divine enablement to consistently pray on behalf of and for others.

P.   To love strangers. The divine enablement to provide fellowship, food, and shelter.

Q.   To stand before. The divine enablement to provide direction, motivation, and vision to God's people.

R.   To translate. The divine enablement to make known the message of one who is speaking in tongues.

S.   To share. The divine enablement to contribute money and other resources to the work of God.

T.   To bring good news. The divine enablement to share the gospel to unbelievers so they respond in faith.

U.   To have compassion. The divine enablement to help those who are suffering or are in need.

V.   To encourage. The divine enablement to present truth so as to strengthen and comfort the discouraged.

W.   To support. The divine enablement to accomplish tasks which free-up and meet the needs of others.

SPIRITUAL GIFTS INVENTORY

Directions:

This is not a test, so there are no wrong answers. The Spiritual Gifts Inventory consists of one hundred and fifteen items. Some items reflect concrete actions; other items are descriptive traits; and still others are statements of belief.

Do not spend too much time on any one item.
Remember that it is not a test.
Usually your immediate response is best.
Do not skip any items.
Do not ask others how they are answering or how they think you should answer.
Work at your own pace.

Record your answers by placing in the blank beside each item the number that corresponds to the answer you want. Mark the extent to which you feel that the item describes you.

Your response choices are:

5 – Highly characteristic of me/definitely true for me

4 – Most of the time this would describe me/be true for me – about 75 percent of the time

3 – Frequently characteristic of me/true for me – about 50 percent of the time

2 – Occasionally characteristic of me/true for me – about 25 percent of the time

1 – Not at all characteristic of me/definitely untrue for me

STATEMENTS

_____ 1.)   I have the ability to organize ideas, resources, time and people effectively.

_____ 2.)   I am willing to study and prepare for the task of teaching.

_____ 3.)   I am able to relate the truths of God to a specific situation.

_____ 4.)   I inspire people to right actions by pointing out the blessings of this path.

_____ 5.)   I have a God-given ability to help others grow in their faith.

_____ 6.)   I possess a special ability to communicate the truth of salvation.

_____ 7.)   I am sensitive to the hurts of people.

_____ 8.)   I experience joy in meeting needs through sharing possessions.

_____ 9.)   I enjoy study.

_____ 10.) I have delivered God's messages of warning and judgment.

_____ 11.) I am able to sense the true motivation of people.

_____ 12.) I trust God in difficult situations.

_____ 13.) I have a strong desire to contribute to the establishment of new churches.

_____ 14.) I feel that God has used me as the agent in a supernatural event.

_____ 15.) I enjoy doing things for people in need.

_____ 16.) I am sensitive to those who suffer physical, mental, or emotional sickness.

_____ 17.) I can delegate and assign meaningful work.

_____ 18.) I have an ability and desire to teach.

_____ 19.) I am usually able to analyze a situation correctly.

_____ 20.) I have a natural tendency to encourage and reward others.

_____ 21.) I am willing to take the initiative in helping other Christians grow in their faith.

_____ 22.) I am unafraid to share with lost people.

_____ 23.) I have an acute awareness of such emotions as loneliness, pain, fear and anger in others.

_____ 24.) I am a cheerful giver.

_____ 25.) I spend time digging into facts.

_____ 26.) I feel that I have a message from God to deliver to others.

_____ 27.) I can recognize when a person is genuine/honest.

_____ 28.) I am willing to yield to God's will rather than question and waver.

_____ 29.) I would like to be more active in getting the gospel to people in other lands.

_____ 30.) It makes me happy to do things for people in need.

_____ 31.) I am willing to be an instrument of healing the physical, emotional, and mental hurts of others.

_____ 32.) I am successful in getting a group to do its work joyfully.

_____ 33.) I have the ability to plan learning approaches.

_____ 34.) I have been able to offer solutions to spiritual problems others are facing.

_____ 35.) I can identify those who need encouragement.

_____ 36.) I have trained Christians to be more obedient disciples of Christ.

_____ 37.) I am willing to do whatever it takes to see others come to Christ.

_____ 38.) I am attracted to people who are hurting.

_____ 39.) I am a generous giver.

_____ 40.) I am able to discover new truths.

_____ 41.) I have spiritual insights from Scripture concerning issues and people that compel me to speak out.

_____ 42.) I can sense when a person is acting in accord with God's will.

_____ 43.) I can trust in God even when things look dark.

_____ 44.) I have a strong desire to take the gospel to places where it has never been heard.

_____ 45.) Others have testified of God's working in miraculous ways in the lives of persons whom I have ministered.

_____ 46.) I enjoy helping people.

_____ 47.) I understand scriptural teachings regarding healing.

_____ 48.) I have been able to make effective and efficient plans for accomplishing the goals of a group.

_____ 49.) I understand the variety of ways people learn.

_____ 50.) I am often consulted when fellow Christians are struggling to make difficult decisions.

_____ 51.) I think about how I can comfort and encourage others.

_____ 52.) I am able to give spiritual direction to others.

_____ 53.) I am able to present the gospel to lost people in such a way that they accept the Lord and His salvation.

_____ 54.) I possess an unusual capacity to understand the feelings of those in distress.

_____ 55.) I have a strong sense of stewardship based on the recognition of God's ownership of all things.

_____ 56.) I know where to get information.

_____ 57.) I have delivered to other people messages that have come directly from God.

_____ 58.) I can sense when a person is acting under God's leadership.

_____ 59.) I try to be in God's will continually.

_____ 60.) I feel that I should take the gospel to people who have different beliefs from me.

_____ 61.) I have the faith to believe that God can do the impossible in a needy situation.

_____ 62.) I love to do things for people.

_____ 63.) I am skilled in setting forth positive and precise steps of action.

_____ 64.) I explain scripture in such a way that others understand it.

_____   44.) I have a strong desire to take the gospel to places where it has never been heard.

_____   65.) I can usually see spiritual solutions to problems.

_____   66.) I am glad when people who need comfort, consolation, encouragement, and counsel seek my help.

_____   67.) I am able to nurture others.

_____   68.) I feel at ease in sharing Christ with nonbelievers.

_____   69.) I recognize the signs of stress and distress in others.

_____   70.) I desire to give generously and unpretentiously to worthwhile projects and ministries.

_____   71.) I can organize facts into meaningful relationships.

_____   72.) God gives me messages to deliver to His people.

_____   73.) I am able to sense whether people are being honest when they tell of their religious experiences.

_____   74.) I try to be available for God to use.

_____   75.) I enjoy presenting the gospel to people of other cultures/backgrounds.

_____   76.) God has used me in miraculous answers to prayer.

_____   77.) I enjoy doing little things that help people.

_____   78.) I can plan a strategy and "bring others aboard."

_____   79.) I can give a clear, uncomplicated presentation.

_____   80.) I have been able to apply biblical truth to the specific needs of my church.

_____   81.) God has used me to encourage others to live Christlike lives.

_____   82.) I have sensed the need to help other people become more effective in their ministries.

_____   83.) I like to talk about Jesus to those who do not know Him.

_____   84.) I have a wide range of study resources.

_____   85.) I feel assured that a situation will change for the glory of God even when the situation seems impossible.

_____   86.) I have an awareness that God still heals people as He did in biblical times.

_____   87.) I enjoy meeting people and helping them to feel welcomed.

_____   88.) I have the ability to speak in a language that I have never learned and do not understand.

_____   89.) I almost always pray in response to the leading of The Holy Spirit, whether understand it or not.

_____   90.) I have the ability to develop strategies or plans to reach identified goals.

_____   91.) I am able to communicate God's truths in a form of art.

_____   92.) I have the ability to respond to a message spoken in tongues by giving an interpretation.

_____   93.) I am able to create a safe and comfortable setting where relationships can develop.

_____   94.) I enjoy working with wood, cloth, paints, metal, glass and other raw materials

_____   95.) I enjoy helping others to become more effective and efficient.

_____   96.) I am able to edify the body of Christ by interpreting a timely message from God.

_____   97.) I am able to develop and use artistic skills such as drama, writing, art, music, etc.

_____   98.) I have the ability to make things which increase the effectiveness of others' ministries

_____   99.) I have the ability to create order out of chaos

_____   100.) I possess the ability to use variety and creativity to captivate people and cause them to consider Christ's message.

_____   101.) I am able to worship the Lord with unknown words too deep for the mind to comprehend.

_____   102.) I often seek ways to connect people together into meaningful relationships.

_____   103.) I enjoy serving with my hands to meet tangible needs

_____ 104.) I have the ability to understand an unlearned language and communicate that message to the body of Christ.

_____ 105.) I enjoy managing or coordinating a variety of responsibilities to accomplish a task

_____ 106.) I am convinced that God moves in direct response to prayer.

_____ 107.) I have the ability to design and build tangible items and resources for ministry use

_____ 108.) I have the ability to set people at ease in unfamiliar surroundings.

_____ 109.) I am able to challenge people's perspective of God through various forms of arts.

_____ 110.) I have the ability to organize people, task, or events.

_____ 111.) I possess a daily awareness to pray for the spiritual battles being waged.

_____ 112.) I am able to work with different kinds of tools and am skilled with my hands.

_____ 113.) I enjoy demonstrating fresh ways to express the Lord's ministry and message.

_____ 114.) I am able to provide an environment where people feel valued and cared for.

_____ 115.) I feel compelled to earnestly pray on behalf of someone or some cause.

SCORING YOUR INVENTORY

Follow these directions to figure your score for each Spiritual Gift.

1.) For each Gift listed below, place in the boxes the number of the responses that you gave to each statement indicated below the boxes.
2.) For each Gift add the numbers in the boxes and put the total in the TOTAL box.
3.) For each Gift divide the TOTAL by the number indicated and place the results in the SCORE box. (Round each number to one decimal place, such as 3.7.) This is your score for the Gift.

Administration
Statements: 90   95   99   105   110   □ ÷ 5 = □
                                                  Total   SCORE

Apostleship
Statements: 13   29   44   60   75   □ ÷ 5 = □
                                                  Total   SCORE

Craftsmanship
Statements: 94   98   103   107   112   □ ÷ 5 = □
                                                  Total   SCORE

Creative Com.
Statements: 91   97   100   109   113   □ ÷ 5 = □
                                                  Total   SCORE

Discernment
Statements: 11   27   42   58   73   □ ÷ 5 = □
                                                  Total   SCORE

Evangelism
Statements: 6   22   37   53   68   83   □ ÷ 6 = □
                                                  Total   SCORE

Exhortation
Statements: 4   20   35   51   66   81   □ ÷ 6 = □
                                                  Total   SCORE

Faith
Statements:

□	□	□	□	□	□	□ ÷ 6 = □
12	28	43	59	74	85	Total SCORE

Giving
Statements:

□	□	□	□	□	□ ÷ 5 = □
8	24	39	55	70	Total SCORE

Healing
Statements:

□	□	□	□	□ ÷ 4 = □
16	31	47	86	Total SCORE

Helps
Statements:

□	□	□	□	□	□ ÷ 5 = □
15	30	46	62	77	Total SCORE

Hospitality
Statements:

□	□	□	□	□	□ ÷ 5 = □
87	93	102	108	114	Total SCORE

Intercession
Statements:

□	□	□	□	□ ÷ 4 = □
89	106	111	115	Total SCORE

Interpretation
Statements:

□	□	□	□ ÷ 3 = □
92	96	104	Total SCORE

Knowledge
Statements:

□	□	□	□	□	□	□ ÷ 6 = □
9	25	40	56	71	84	Total SCORE

Leadership
Statements:

□	□	□	□	□	□	□ ÷ 6 = □
1	17	32	48	63	78	Total SCORE

Mercy
Statements:

□	□	□	□	□	□ ÷ 5 = □
7	23	38	54	69	Total SCORE

Miracles
Statements: □   □   □   □   □ ÷ 4 = □
             14   45   61   76   Total   SCORE

Prophecy
Statements: □   □   □   □   □   □ ÷ 5 = □
             10   26   41   57   72   Total   SCORE

Shepherding
Statements: □   □   □   □   □   □   □ ÷ 6 = □
             5   21   36   52   67   82   Total   SCORE

Teaching
Statements: □   □   □   □   □   □   □ ÷ 6 = □
             2   18   33   49   64   79   Total   SCORE

Tongues
Statements: □   □   □ ÷ 2 = □
             88   101   Total   SCORE

Wisdom
Statements: □   □   □   □   □   □   □ ÷ 6 = □
             3   19   34   50   65   80   Total   SCORE

GRAPHING YOUR PROFILE

1.) For each Gift place a mark on the bar at the point that corresponds to your SCORE for that Gift.
2.) For each Gift shade the bar below the mark that you have drawn.
3.) The resultant graph gives a picture of your Gifts. Gifts for which the bars are long are the ones in which you appear to be the strongest. Gifts for which the bars are very short are the ones in which you appear not to be as strong.

SCORE

Score					Gift
5.0 4.0 3.0 2.0 1.0 0.0					WISDOM
					TONGUES
					TEACHING
					SHEPHERDING
					PROPHECY
					MIRACLES
					MERCY
					LEADERSHIP
					KNOWLEDGE
					INTERPRETATION of TONGUES
					INTERCESSORY PRAYER
					HOSPITALITY
					HELPS
					HEALING
					GIVING
					FAITH
					EXHORTATION
					EVANGELISM
					DISCERNMENT
					CREATIVE COMMUNICATION
					CRAFTSMANSHIP
					APOSTLESHIP
					ADMINISTRATION

41

SEVEN INDICATORS FOR DETERMINING YOUR PASSION

Directions:

To help identify your passion or heart's desire, as defined on page 75 of your textbook, answer the following questions.

1.) What would cause you to eagerly jump out of bed in the morning?

_____

_____

_____

2.) What image strikes an emotional chord with you?

_____

_____

_____

3.) What are your most enjoyable achievements?

_____

_____

_____

4.) What do you become preoccupied with, or focused on most?

_____

_____

_____

5.) What's happening when you feel you are making a difference?

_____

_____

_____

6.) What energizes you?

_____

_____

_____

7.) How does your passion glorify God and edify others?

_____

_____

_____

PERSONAL STYLE ASSESSMENT – PART I
HOW ARE YOU ORGANIZED?

DIRECTIONS

1.) For each statement and its response, rate the perspective with 1 indicating the least amount of interest and 5 indicating the greatest amount of interest.
2.) Do not answer according to what you feel is expected by a spouse, family member, employer, etc. but select the behavior or perspective that would come naturally to you if you knew there were no restrictions on or consequences for your personal expression.
3.) Total both rating scale columns (1&2) and write rating scale totals in the blank provided at the end of each column.

STATEMENT BEGINNING	RESPONSE #1	RATING SCALE #1	RESPONSE #2	RATING SCALE #2
While on vacation I prefer to:	be spontaneous	1 2 3 4 5	follow a set plan	1 2 3 4 5
I prefer to set guidelines that are:	general	1 2 3 4 5	specific	1 2 3 4 5
I prefer to:	leave my options open	1 2 3 4 5	settle things now	1 2 3 4 5
I prefer projects that have:	variety	1 2 3 4 5	routine	1 2 3 4 5
I like to:	play it by ear	1 2 3 4 5	stick to a plan	1 2 3 4 5
I find routine:	boring	1 2 3 4 5	restful	1 2 3 4 5
I accomplish tasks best:	by working it out as I go	1 2 3 4 5	by following a plan	1 2 3 4 5
	Add up the responses in the rating scale #1 column. Place your total score in the box to your right.	Rating scale column#1 total _____	**Add up the responses in the rating scale #2 column. Place your total score in the box to your right.**	Rating scale column#2 total _____

Enter your highest score here. ☐   **How Are You Organized?**

How Are You Organized?   If your highest score was from the rating scale #1 column, write in the blank above "How are you organized," **UNSTRUCTURED.** If your highest score was from the rating scale #2 column, write in that same blank space **STRUCTURED.**

PERSONAL STYLE ASSESSMENT – PART II

HOW ARE YOU ENERGIZED?

DIRECTIONS

1.) For each statement and its response, rate the perspective with 1 indicating the least amount of interest and 5 indicating the greatest amount of interest.

2.) Do not answer according to what you feel is expected by a spouse, family member, employer, etc. but select the behavior or perspective that would come naturally to you if you knew there were no restrictions on or consequences for your personal expression.

3.) Total both rating scale columns (1&2) and write rating scale totals in the blank provided at the end of each column.

STATEMENT BEGINNING	RESPONSE #1	RATING SCALE #1					RESPONSE #2	RATING SCALE #2				
I'm comfortable:	doing things for people	1	2	3	4	5	being with people	1	2	3	4	5
When doing a task, I tend to:	focus on the goal	1	2	3	4	5	focus on relationships	1	2	3	4	5
I get excited about:	advancing a cause	1	2	3	4	5	creating community	1	2	3	4	5
I feel I've accomplished something when I've:	gotten a job done	1	2	3	4	5	built a relationship	1	2	3	4	5
It is important to start a meeting:	on time	1	2	3	4	5	when everyone gets there	1	2	3	4	5
I'm concerned with:	meeting a deadline	1	2	3	4	5	maintaining the team	1	2	3	4	5
I place a higher value on:	action	1	2	3	4	5	communication	1	2	3	4	5
	Add up the responses in the rating scale #1 column. Place your total score in the box to your right.	Rating scale column #1 total _____					**Add up the responses in the rating scale #2 column. Place your total score in the box to your right.**	Rating scale column #2 total _____				

Enter your highest score here. ☐   How Are You Energized?

How Are You Organized?   If your highest score was from the rating scale #1 column, write in the blank above "How are you energized," **TASK ORIENTED.**
If your highest score was from the rating scale #2 column, write in that same blank space **PEOPLE ORIENTED.**

STUDY QUESTIONS – CHAPTER 5

1.) List the four prerequisites for discovering your Spiritual Gifts.

_______________ _______________

_______________ _______________

2.) List the key factors involved with discovery of your Spiritual Gifts.

_______________ _______________

_______________ _______________

3.) What is the difference between a burning desire and willingness?

____

4.) What do the scriptures say about motives as it relates to Spiritual Gifts?

____

5.) What does the author mean when he refers to "the wagon"?

____

6.) Spiritual Gifts are only given by God to _______________ _______________ _______________.

7.) Where does discernment come from? _______________

8.) What does the acronym SHAPE stand for?

S – _______________
H – _______________
A – _______________
P – _______________
E – _______________

9.) What are the three areas of passion when it comes to desire?

_______________ _______________ _______________

10.) What is meant by the terms "Gift mix" and "ministry profile"?

____

11.) What is the main purpose of the Parable of the Pounds in Luke 19:20-24?

____

12.) How did Jesus demonstrate the great lesson of servanthood in John 13: 12-14?

____

Answers on page 66

6

Developing & Using Your Spiritual Gifts

Hindrances to Discovery & Development of Spiritual Gifts

Unconfessed and Unresolved Sin

A Fruitless Vessel

A Spirit of Fear

Lack of Involvement

Shallow Spiritual Capacity

PREPARATION AND PLANNING

Directions:

Write down your plans for using your Spiritual Gift(s) using the chart below. To better understand preparation and planning refer to pages 87-88 of textbook.

MY OVERALL PLAN	I PLAN TO ...
My Ministry Profile	Utilize my Gift(s)of: _____, Passion(s) for: _____, & my Personal Style of: _____ as follows:
My Three Month Goal is to:	
My One Year Goal is to:	
My Long Range Goal is to:	

PRACTICE AND EXPERIMENT

Directions:

<u>List Your Gift Mix</u>: Fit your Gifts in the appropriate Gift mix section in the chart above using one or more of the following descriptions below: To better understand Gift mix, refer to page 77 of textbook.

1.) This chart consist of Gifts dealing with outreach and evangelism, resulting in the numerical growth of the Church.

	Evangelism	Tongues
	Miracles	Interpretation of Tongues
	Healing	Voluntary Poverty
	Mercy	Deliverance

2.) This chart consist of Gifts dealing with the spiritual maturity of the Church. These are Gifts fostering spiritual growth, providing discipleship training and membership support.

	Prophecy	Exhortation and Encouragement
	Teaching	Discernment of Spirits
	Pastor/Shepherd	Faith
	Knowledge	Intercessory Prayer
	Wisdom	Hospitality

3.) This chart consist of Gifts dealing with the administrative functions of the Church, such as, financial management, maintenance of physical facilities, and membership support.

	Leadership	Administration
	Helps	Service
	Giving	

DEVELOPING A SPIRITUAL GIFT (A CASE STUDY)

Directions:
Use the chart below for a Gift you know you have and make a plan for developing that Gift. To better understand the purpose of this case study, refer to page 95 of textbook.

STEP	PROCEDURES	FOLLOW-UP SUGGESTIONS
1 Develop a clear understanding of the basic principles of biblical: _____ (Gift)	➤ Find and study scripture to support your Gift. ➤ Study biblical characters who exemplified your Gift.	List scripture references pertaining to your Gift: _____ _____ _____ List biblical characters with your Gift: _____ _____ _____
2 Develop a system of study or plan of action on: _____ (Gift)	➤ Study weekly scripture lessons on your Gift. ➤ Memorize scriptures on your Gift. ➤ Volunteer to use your Gift.	List books and other references on your Gift: _____ _____ Memorize at least one scripture and write it here: _____ _____ _____ Define how you can use your Gift right now: _____ _____
3 Practice the principles of _____ (Gift) you are learning with your family and on your job.	➤ Define the traits of the Gift.	Ask others to evaluate your usage of the Gift in your daily life. 4
4 Perfect People Skills	➤ Concentrate on areas where your Gift might be useful.	List how people skills may be necessary in these areas when using your Gift. _____ _____
5 Choose a Mentor	➤ Ask a leader you admire to serve as your mentor.	List persons you may consider to be your mentor then narrow it down to one person. _____ _____ _____

STUDY QUESTIONS – CHAPTER 6

1.) What is the main point of the biblical teaching on Spiritual Gifts?

_____

2.) List five hindrances to developing your Spiritual Gifts.

_____ _____

_____ _____

_____

3.) What is meant by the term "spiritual capacity"?

_____

_____

4.) List the steps required to develop a Gift-based ministry.

_____ _____

_____ _____

5.) _____ is the key to success and _____ is the key to failure.

6.) List three people who were known to have prepared well for their ministry.

_____ _____

_____

7.) How did Paul prepare for his ministry?

_____

8.) What is the best way to combat ignorance about Spiritual Gifts? _____

9) Which strong emotion often results from lack of knowledge? _____

Answers on page 66

7

Mentoring
Spiritual Gifts

Why Christian Mentoring?

Christian mentoring in the Church today is needed.

Younger saints need to learn from more seasoned saints how to:
- walk in love
- exhibit Christ-like behavior
- give to the poor
- watch, fast and pray
- operate in the Gifts of The Spirit

WHERE ARE YOU IN CHRISTIAN MENTORING?

Directions:
Answer the following questions to determine where you are in mentoring.

1.)   Do you currently participate in a Christian mentoring relationship? Circle: Yes or No

2.)   Are you the mentor or the mentoree? _____
        If you are the mentor, then you needn't answer the remainder of these questions.

3.)   As a potential mentor, make a list of persons you know who would benefit from a one-on-
        one relationship in which you could share your practical knowledge of Spiritual Gifts. After
        making the list, take the time to pray about God leading you in mentoring this or these
        relationships.

        _____   _____

        _____   _____

4.)   As a potential mentoree who is not being mentored, begin to concentrate on the benefits
        of mentoring. Next, take time to pray about God leading you into a Christian mentoring
        relationship, as well as pray about the potential mentors you listed earlier at the end of the
        activity on page 50.

        _____

        _____

STUDY QUESTIONS – CHAPTER 7

1.) What is mentoring?

_____

_____

_____

2.) Mentoring forces sharing of _____ _____.

3.) Where did the term mentoring originate?

_____

4.) What does the scripture tell us about mentoring in Matthew 28?

_____

5.) Who was Jesus' mentor? _____

6.) How does Proverbs 27:17 relate to mentoring?

_____

_____

7.) List one of the four advantages of developing Spiritual Gifts using mentoring relationships?

_____

8.) List the six steps to starting a Gift-Based Ministry in your church.

_____   _____

_____   _____

_____   _____

Answers on page 67

Starting a Gift-Based Ministry in Your Church

Gift-Based Ministry Defined

A Gift-Based Ministry is a ministry in which all members serve God by employing their God-given Spiritual Gifts in the most effective and pleasurable way.

"Playing Church" Defined

"Playing Church" is defined as going through the traditional motions of a particular church, social order or religious organization without receiving the power of God to work effectively therein.

The Importance of Spiritual Gifts in the Church of God

Spiritual Gifts are vital to the effectiveness of the Church of God in the world today and tomorrow.

12 Steps to Starting a Gift-Based Ministry (Pastors and Saints)

STEP 1	Believe It
STEP 2	Receive It
STEP 3	Study It
STEP 4	Preach It
STEP 5	Model & Mirror It
STEP 6	Teach It
STEP 7	Reveal It (Go Public)
STEP 8	Provide for It
STEP 9	Encourage It – Support It
STEP 10	Reinforce It
STEP 11	Glorify God with It
STEP 12	Thank Him for It & Praise Him for It

STUDY QUESTIONS – CHAPTER 8

1.)   Define the term "Gift-Based Ministry."

_____

_____

2.)   What does the author mean by "playing church"?

_____

3.)   List four advantages of a Gift-Based Ministry.

_____   _____

_____   _____

4.)   What should you do if your church is not a Gift-Based Ministry?

_____

_____

_____

5.)   If you are a Pastor, list the twelve steps to starting a Gift-Based Ministry.

_____

_____

_____

_____

_____

_____

_____

_____

_____

_____

_____

_____

Answers on page 67

9

A Special
Word & Gift
for Singles

Celebrating Celibacy
The best way to handle celibacy is to celebrate it!!!

The Gift of Celibacy

Did you know that Celibacy is a Gift from God?

Paul did not expect that all singles would be able to remain single. It is a Gift of God. It is a proper Gift. A person must be spiritually Gifted of God to be able to be single and remain single and without sin as a result of that singleness.

What did Jesus say about Celibacy?

Jesus said ... Not all can accept this word, but only those to whom it is granted. Some are incapable of marriage because they were born so; some, because they were made so by others; some, because they have renounced marriage for the sake of the Kingdom of God.

Whoever can accept this ought to accept it. —Matthew 19: 11-12.

STUDY QUESTIONS – CHAPTER 9

1.) What does Paul mean when he mentions a "Proper Gift"?

_____

2.) What is meant in the scripture by the term "be fruitful and multiply"?

_____

3.) Why are singles more apt to seek moral and spiritual direction?

_____

_____

4.) What did Jesus say about celibacy?

_____

_____

_____

5.) How is celibacy a Gift?

_____

_____

Answers on page 68

ANSWERS TO STUDY QUESTIONS

CHAPTER 1
1.) The greatest Gift of all Gifts and the one that sparks all other Gifts is the Gift of love.
2.) The chapter declares that you may have all the other Gifts, but if you do not have the Gift of love you really don't have anything. Furthermore, when all the other Gifts have failed or passed away, only the Gift of love will be left standing.
3.) (1) Love is patient, (2) love is expressed in kindness, (3) love rejoices in truth, (4) love protects and endures, (5) love trusts, (6) love hopes, and (7) love perseveres
4.) (1) Love is not envious or jealous, (2) love is not boastful, (3) love is not proud, (4) love does not act rude, (5) love is not self-seeking, (6) love does not easily get mad, (7) love does not keep score of wrongs, and (8) love does not rejoice in evil or weakness.
5.) (1) love, (2) love, (3) covers, sin, (4) what God has prepared for those who love Him, (5) follow love, (6) the Gift, fruit, (7) fear, (8) love
6.) Gift, fruit
7.) You will stir up all the Spiritual Gifts of God.
8.) Fear will control your life.
9.) Any sacrifice done out of love; giving until it hurts.
10.) They were given by God for the increase of the Body of Christ.

CHAPTER 2
1.) Spirit of fear
2.) love
3.) Since perfect love casts out fear, and intimidation is caused by fear, intimidation can be overcome through the love of God.
4.) Satan sends the spirit of fear.
5.) We can bind or restrain Satan.
6.) Identify three areas where you rest in your own comfort zone ...
7.) It leaves you vulnerable to the enemy.
8.) To starve the flesh means to deprive the flesh of the Sodom and Gomorrah locations and Babylon associations, watching what you read and who you listen to and associate with. To feed the spirit means to feast more on the Word of God in order to strengthen your spirit while at the same time weakening the flesh.
9.) Snakes cannot survive above a certain altitude. The analogy made refers to fighting the adversary on the level of love and prayer rather than on the lower level of the flesh. You cannot overcome the devil with ground level (carnal) weapons. But if you take the battle up to the higher level of love he simply cannot exist.
10.) Hollywood Christianity is religious entertainment. It is glamorizing Church and Christianity. It deceives the Christian into believing that all that glitters is gold.
11.) A Popeye Mentality says, "That's all I can stands and I can't stands no more." He would eat his spinach (The Holy Spirit) and defeat his enemy.
12.) He was being intimidated. Although Timothy had a great faith, something in his ministry had gone awry. His witness had grown cold. His boldness had been lost. Timothy had become timid. Timothy was experiencing timidity.

CHAPTER 3

1.) They may lay dormant, latent, become unemployed, wrongly employed, go into recession, or like an older soldier, simply fade away, but they do not die.
2.) To bring people of God to life again.
3.) The Holy Spirit.
4.) The bones represent the Spiritual Gifts that are dry and dormant in the lives of believers in the Church. With The Holy Spirit's help, these Gifts can be revived and made alive again.
5.) One.
6.) The Holy Spirit is the power behind all Spiritual Gifts.

CHAPTER 4

1.) A steward is one who manages something that does not belong to him.
2.) To be a faithful minister of whatever God has entrusted to you.
3.) Acknowledgment – One must acknowledge that God is the source, owner and giver of all Gifts.

Reconciliation – One must always be reconciled to God and to others in order to be a good steward of God's Gifts.

Availability – One must recognize that time, Gifts/talents and money belong to God. Availability means allowing time in our busy schedule to be available to be used by God.

Motivation – Your reason for serving God must be to demonstrate your love, thanksgiving and obedience to God rather than to be recognized by people.

Spiritual Maturity – To fulfill all of God's purposes for you in the church.

Sacrifice – Sacrifice means giving up something of ourselves for the benefit of others or for a greater cause.

Accountability – We will be held accountable for the use we make of our Spiritual Gifts. There will be a believer's judgment wherein every man's work will be judged.

Faithfulness – We must be faithful to use and not neglect the Spiritual Gifts that God has entrusted to us.
4.) In the Parable of the Pounds and in the Parable of the Talents, Jesus makes it clear that if stewards do not neglect their Gifts, they will be rewarded for their faithfulness.
5.) God gives us Spiritual Gifts so that we can serve him and each other. It is the initial motivation and it must also be the end result.

CHAPTER 5

1.) You must be a Christian. You must believe the Word of God that says that God has given Spiritual Gifts for the church today. You must offer yourself to the Lord. You must pray.

2.) Key factors are discernment, a burning desire, a willing attitude and the right motive.

3.) You may have a burning desire but if you are unwilling to go when God calls because of fear or some other hindrance, you will not go.

4.) Without the right motives, everything is canceled. The Gifts just will not be effective and God's Will, will not be done.

5.) It represents Christ, the victor, awarding Gifts to the Church. The wagon represents a "wagon load" of Gifts that Jesus gave to the church.

6.) Born again believers.

7.) God gives us discernment when we ask for it.

8.) S – *Spiritual Gifts*, H – *Heart*, A – *Abilities*, P – *Personal Temperament*, E – *Experience*.

9.) People, Roles & Functions, and Causes.

10.) Your different Gifts determine your Gift mix. Your ministry profile includes not only your Gift, but also your passion and God-given personality style.

11.) If stewards of God's Gifts do not neglect these Gifts, they will be rewarded for their faithfulness.

12.) He washed the disciple's feet.

CHAPTER 6

1.) Gifts are to be used, and if they are to be used best, they must be developed.

2.) Unconfessed and unresolved sin – Fruitlessness – The Spirit of Fear – Lack of Involvement – Shallow Spiritual Capacity.

3.) The ability to carry The Spirit of God, live in hard spiritual climates when others run, allowing your character and spirit to be prepared to do God's will, to persevere when others settle, and the ability to carry God's Glory.

4.) (1) preparation and planning, (2) study and meditation, (3) practice and experimentation, and (4) using your Gift in ministry.

5.) Planning, failing to plan.

6.) Luke, Paul, and Jesus.

7.) He conferred with God and spent three years preparing himself in Arabia. Afterwards he went to Jerusalem to see Peter and abode with him fifteen days.

8.) The best way to combat ignorance is with study.

9.) Fear.

CHAPTER 7

1.) Mentoring is a cooperative and nurturing relationship between a seasoned proven person, and a less experienced novice who wants to learn and gain valuable practical information and insight into the particular God-given expertise of the more experienced person.

2.) Practical information.

3.) In Greek Mythology. The story of Mentor comes from Homer's Odyssey.

4.) The Great Commission is a biblical command to mentor (make disciples).

5.) God Himself chose to be a mentor to Jesus.

6.) "Iron sharpeneth iron; as a man sharpeneth the countenance of his friend." It deals with the influence which men have on each other whether positive or negative. Mentoring is a relationship where one influences another.

7.) Mentorees become Mentors.

8.) (1) Get senior Pastor and Church leadership support, (2) Create opportunities for relationship development, (3) Determine how mentors and mentorees are going to be selected, (4) Train the mentors, (5) Name it and go public and (6) Select, appoint and assign a mentoring coordinator.

CHAPTER 8

1.) A continuous ministry of the church that expects all the members of the body to actively participate in a life-long ministry task of service based on their Spiritual Gifts used mostly effectively and pleasurably.

2.) Just going through the motions of church and being religious. Not taking the things of God seriously.

3.) (1) Eliminating random selection of workers in the church, (2) Mobilizing volunteers for service, (3) Keeping the fire burning and, (4) Opening the front door wider and closing the back door tighter.

4.) You should identify and develop your own Spiritual Gifts and join and existing ministry in your church immediately. If there is no existing ministry in your local church that matches your Gift mix, then meet with the pastor and ask permission to start one.

5.) Believe it – Receive it – Study it – Preach it – Model & Mirror it – Teach it – Reveal it (go public) – Provide for it – Encourage & Support it – Reinforce it – Glorify God with it – Praise and Thank Him for it

CHAPTER 9

1.) Paul refers to the proper Gift as being a Gift which is a sufficient Gift and uniquely fashioned for a particular person and a particular time.

2.) The term refers to human race multiplying and replenishing the earth rather than to individuals.

3.) Because in their situation, they are alone with no companion to talk to and get direction from. They are more in need of fellowship, spiritual connectedness and emotional intimacy.

4.) "Not all can accept this word, but only those to whom it is granted. Some are incapable of marriage because they were born so; some, because they were made so by others; some, because they have renounced marriage for the sake of the kingdom of God. Whoever can accept this ought to accept it." (Matt. 19:11-12).

5.) Paul did not expect that all singles would be able to remain single. It is a Gift of God. It is a proper Gift. A person must be spiritually Gifted of God to be able to be single and remain single and without sin as a result of that singleness.

SERVANT PROFILE SHEET

Name _____
               Last   Firs

Address _____
                  Street   Apt. #

_____ _____ _____
        City   State   Zip

Home Phone ( ) _____ Work Phone ( ) _____

PAST MINISTRY SERVICE:

    Ministry _____   Position _____

    Ministry _____   Position _____

    Ministry _____   Position _____

SERVANT PROFILE

SPIRITUAL GIFT(S): _____ _____ _____

PASSION(S): _____ _____ _____

Talents, Special Skills, Abilities: _____ _____

_____ _____ _____

PERSONAL STYLE: ___ structured ___ unstructured ___ task oriented ___ people oriented

AVAILABILITY:

	MORNING	AFTERNOON	EVENING	ANYTIME
SUNDAY				
MONDAY				
TUESDAY				
WEDNESDAY				
THURSDAY				
FRIDAY				
SATURDAY				
ANY DAY				

COURSE EVALUATION

STIR UP THE GIFTS MATERIAL

1.) To what extent did the textbook and workbook/study guide meet your expectations in terms of value and quality?

5	4	3	2	1
Went Beyond Expectations		Met Expectations		Less than Expected

2.) How much learning did you experience from this course?

5	4	3	2	1
Significant		Moderate		Little

3.) Would you recommend that others take this course?

5	4	3	2	1
Yes Definitely		Possibly		Definitely Not

4.) What aspects of this program were most useful?

_____

_____

5.) What aspects of this program were least useful?

_____

_____

STIR UP THE GIFTS INSTRUCTOR

6.) To what extent did the instructor demonstrate depth of understanding and credibility with regard to the material?

5	4	3	2	1
To a very great extent		To some extent		To little or no extent

7.) To what extent did the instructor's interaction with the participants facilitate your learning?

5	4	3	2	1
To a very great extent		To some extent		To little or no extent

- -

8.) What, if anything, should have been included in this curriculum that was not?

_____

_____